THE UNSEEN FUNDRAISER

*Lessons, Life and Laughs
from a Small Shop Finesser*

TANYA PIETRKOWSKI

TP Strategies, LLC
Chicago, 2026

ISBN: 979-8-9937018-0-6
Library of Congress Control Number: 2026902624

Front cover image and illustrations by Lily Freedman
Book design by Benjamin Schneider

First edition 2026

Published by TP Strategies, LLC
tpstrategies.biz
Chicago, IL

The stories and reflections in this book are based on the author's experiences. Identifying details are changed as needed to protect privacy.

For bulk orders, permissions, or speaking requests, contact tpietr@yahoo.com

Table of Contents

Preface

This book is for the scrappy ones with boots-on-the-ground—small-shop fundraisers, nonprofit founders wearing twelve hats, and board members who aren't afraid to get their hands dirty to keep the mission alive. If that's you, you already know what I mean. In this sector, big institutions get the spotlight and the budgets. But the small ones? They get things done with duct tape, grit, and determination. I've lived that life. I've stuffed the envelopes, put out the fires, written the grants, and swept the floors. Now I focus my consulting work on the underdogs—because that's where my heart lives.

This is a collection of real-life reflections—plus my favorite chicken recipe—for anyone trying to make it work, day in and day out. It's a look behind the curtain at the humor, hustle, chaos, and heart that keep missions going. Others will do a better job in teaching the step-by-step of fundraising.

If you're feeling burned out, stuck, or overlooked, I hope something here reminds you that your work matters. That you matter. And if something resonates, reach out—I'd love to keep the conversation going.

Introduction:
Why I Am Writing This Book Right Now

After 25+ years working in nonprofit—ten of them at one organization—I finally stepped away to reflect, recalibrate, and share some big-picture impressions of what I've learned. I've always viewed fundraisers from small shops as the unseen and underestimated. We learn to juggle it all, putting out one fire while another flares up. We're the ones covered in the grit of the job, quietly driving support of all sizes.

Whether you're new to the field or transitioning mid-career, I hope these reflections—on a sector that can be deeply political and stodgy at its worst, and transformational at its best—will feel validating, eye-opening, irreverent, and comical. This book is about what I want to do next. And honestly, that's a big deal for me. Fundraisers are trained to be endlessly accommodating to organizations, boards, donors, colleagues, and causes. We're the people-pleasers who know how to read a room; who smile and nod; who close the gift and say "thank you" with sincerity and strategy. Fundraising is a gift, and it's meant for people-whisperers with gold-level soft skills. I've always been that person. Then the pandemic happened and I felt those skills being stifled inside a single institution. So, I left, determined to use my people-gift in more meaningful ways.

Now, I work across causes, campaigns, and communities—some as paid opportunities, some as volunteer. I've been lucky to witness the moments that matter most to me:

- Coaching others to speak up—and witnessing them rise
- Supporting organizations in crisis—reminding them of their resilience
- Raising real money—because when giving is meaningful, it lasts
- Volunteering on a Chicago aldermanic campaign—we lost, but I found my local spark
- Attending national social justice conferences—feeling the fire of shared purpose
- Walking the halls of Springfield, IL and Washington, D.C.—watching bold ideas grow
- Helping artists pitch their work—because art deserves investment
- Encouraging founders—reminding them they're not crazy, just tired
- Drinking gasoline-grade coffee while my pudgy cat Finn supervises
- Failing at exercises—and learning to laugh in the process

I could only reflect on these moments after stepping off the nonprofit hamster wheel. Letting go of the competitive grind has made me a better fundraiser, a greater connector, and a happier version of myself in the long run.

My goal now is to say "yes" to what matters. To

embrace discomfort and stay curious. To build deeper relationships. To offer insight without needing to run the whole show or engage in the daily administrative tasks that brought me down. And to work in ways that feel rooted rather than rushed.

Everything I do now is connected to the relationships I built early in my career. I carry those lessons with me with every step forward.

Thanks for connecting with me.

Finding My Groove:
Reflections from the Nonprofit Trenches

My high school mentor, the late Lt. Colonel Phil Turner, once told our class that by the time you hit 50, you start caring more about the impact you're making than how high you can climb the career ladder. He was right—at least in my case.

After more than a decade at a nonprofit I loved, with many goals checked off, I found myself increasingly drawn to side projects that spoke more deeply to my spirit. Once my daughter graduated college and my husband changed careers, I finally had the space to ask: What do I want to do?

It was then that I left my comfortable job to move into consulting.

With that freedom came clarity. Metrics like dollars raised or income earned mattered less than the meaning and purpose of the work. I still care about results, but I've come to value joy and presence in my work over chasing targets. Some of the best fundraising happens when you stop leading with the quest for money and start connecting more deeply with the purpose.

Success is more than numbers on a spreadsheet. It's keeping the mission alive by leaving the doors open one more day. In this field, faith and vision are the primary drivers of success.

We're taught to admire the big-dollar shops, when it's often the small teams that do more with less—and create a deeper, more lasting impact as a result. Fundraisers thrive where they can be themselves. I found my place somewhere between two tribes: lawyers and artists. Having spent over 60% of my career working alongside attorneys, I've come to appreciate their sharp, tactical mindset. We balance each other: my big-picture thinking, their precise execution.

At the heart of it all is connection. I'll always choose people over short-term performance. When you shift your mindset about success, self-worth, and what really matters, your work improves—and the money follows.

This book is here to help you work beyond professional obstacles like bad bosses, finicky donors, overwhelming workloads, and self-doubt—and to teach you to define success on your own terms.

PART I

Advice for the Small Shop Fundraiser or Nonprofit Founder

There is Room for All of Us in Fundraising:
Define Success for Yourself

Fundraising can come naturally to those who enjoy it, yet it remains challenging even when executed successfully, because we are dealing with human emotions. Understanding when and how to make the ask is an art form. Fundraisers use their skills of discretion, listening, and ethical judgment with every relationship and funding opportunity. Note that leadership and management skills differ from sales skills and warrant the time and space to be developed separately.

Fundraisers often take their sales skills too seriously—largely because everyone else tends to be uncomfortable asking for money. Here's a secret: A great sense of humor serves as a major asset, because you just may have to do any task that arises to get to the finish line in this work. No matter how perfectly you plan, "Sales with a mission" is always unpredictable. Your adaptability will be tested.

Know What You Need to Thrive

I rebelled against early mentors who prioritized artificial sentiment and overly-polished donor interactions. I thrived when I could be my full self and felt supported.

I had to discover the right environment—one that valued my fearlessness, individuality, and ingenuity. Surprisingly, I found that the legal aid sector is a small, tight-knit niche. It was a blank canvas, wide open for creative fundraising. Over time, I became a leading fundraising expert in this space.

I was once warned professionally, "If you plan events, no one will take you seriously as a fundraiser." Ironically, strategic event planning became my hallmark. Events allowed me to advance missions, sharpen messaging, and spotlight organizations that struggled to tell their own stories. While I'll write grants if I'm the best person for the story, I often defer to others who enjoy it more. I prefer to focus on strategy and connecting people.

Fundraising is a Team Sport

Fundraising success relies on a wide range of skills—and it's essential to respect what others bring to the table. Even when you are the one making the ask, you are first and foremost part of a greater team that includes researchers, strategists, communicators, volunteers, and other staff who all contribute.

At one organization, I cultivated a quiet donor who became one of our largest supporters. I left before the gift was finalized, but I'm proud of the role I played. That's teamwork.

I'm impressed by both massive campaigns and first-time fundraisers working in small nonprofits. Leadership is undefined by the budget size of the organization.

Fundraising takes all kinds: data analysts, big-picture strategists, hesitant executive directors, persistent board members, grant writers, creatives, admin staff, tech consultants, auditors, and financial managers. Every role matters.

Ignore the Naysayers.

I've worked under difficult managers and inefficient systems. Elitist fundraisers who look down on small shops frustrate me most.

Two consultants once told me it was impossible to raise $1 million for an anniversary campaign. After we exceeded our goal, I sent them both thank-you notes—for underestimating us.

If you're a fundraiser or founder, push the "no"s out of your way. Drive with your faith and conviction to move forward.

Find Self Validation in Your Work, from the Beginning

My first professional fundraising job was with the Girl Scouts in central Illinois, right after I had my daughter in the mid-'90s. They were advertising for a capital campaign coordinator, and honestly, it sounded way over my head. I wrote a genuine letter, admitting I lacked experience and expressed my enthusiasm to rise to the challenge. They hired me.

I spent a wonderful year learning under a development director who was a habitual smoker with emphysema and who hated camping. She was one of the best strategists I've ever worked with. When I relocated to Chicago, the Girl Scouts eventually hired an experienced consulting firm to finish the campaign to build a new dining hall at Camp Tapawingo. I probably raised just $30,000 out of the $1 million goal—and I learned so much in the process. Even as a novice, I knew I loved the work.

Back in Chicago, I had some dreadful interviews where a few fundraisers insulted my experience and enthusiasm. I was even made to cry in one interview, and I found the team to be great hypocrites from a mission and professional perspective. The head and nastiest fundraiser at one place ended up leaving the organization, for which I like to believe that karma was a factor.

I had to reflect on why I wanted to be part of a world that sometimes placed wealth and polish above values. But deep down, I knew that my purpose was to bring hope and connection to others. Fundraising is one way to do that.

Next, I landed at a Jewish day camp and daycare organization in Chicago on another capital campaign assignment. It was an entry-level job where I quickly realized I was performing more administrative tasks than anything else. After 18 months, I left in search of a more demanding fundraising role.

Over time, I developed a thicker skin. I believe everyone deserves dignity, regardless of who they are or where they come from. You may have heard the saying that the folks you meet on the way up are also the folks you meet on the way down. You're also likely to cross paths with the same people in your field repeatedly. I take this philosophy seriously. I treat everyone interested in fundraising and communications as professionals working to grow through their experiences.

Those early bad experiences shaped me into a better mentor. I now make it a mission to spot potential in others and help them grow toward their interests and talents. I once interviewed five candidates for a development associate role and offered them feedback after the interview. One young woman took me up on my offer and was eager to learn. I helped her apply to a fellowship program where she received mentorship; eventually, she became a grant writer and moved up in her career even further after that. I served as a reference when she landed the first job—and from there, she was launched.

In other cases, I've met incredible communicators who disliked asking for money. I helped them see that they can contribute more meaningfully by focusing on communication. Great storytelling, branding, and strategic messaging are also vital to development. There's room for many voices in this work, and many personalities—including mine.

The abuse I experienced in those early jobs and interviews motivated me to be better at my job, as a mentor and ally. I make it a point to bring people in from a variety of backgrounds with all kinds of talents into this work. We are richer for it.

The Rumpelstiltskin Fallacy and the Gift of Underestimated Assets

A friend once told me she used to think fundraising was just about asking for money—or hiring someone with a magical Rolodex (list of contacts, for those unfamiliar with an actual Rolodex) to open the right doors. I've heard this often from folks unfamiliar with the fundraising process.

Yes, some people have impressive networks. And they'll be the first to admit that relationships—even more than institutions—drive results. The golden rule of fundraising? It's people asking people and recognizing that the mission comes first from the staff perspective.

As a fundraiser, my role often involves building relationships, making connections, working behind the scenes, and ensuring the right person is asking. Sometimes they say "yes"; sometimes they say "no." It always starts with the base of the relationships at hand. And sometimes, the relationship itself is more valuable than the gift.

Still, I often hear from organizations just starting out: "Can you make introductions for us?" They imagine I'm Rumpelstiltskin, spinning gold from straw. What I tell them is this: You already have what you need. You're sitting on a wealth of relationship assets. The key is focusing—strategically—on how you identify and nurture them.

Success should be defined by the people doing the work rather than having a definition imposed by outside experts.

I once had a consultant pitch me a proposal. I told her clearly: We need help solving one specific problem at the time. But instead of focusing, she served up the whole enchilada—at a price and amount of labor that was way beyond our capacity. Even though my board president was intrigued, it was a non-starter. Why? Because she didn't listen. She overlooked the internal customer—me.

I always begin by identifying what an organization already has—not just what's missing. In this work, we're knocked down often. It's easy to get stuck on what's lacking. But we have to start from a place of abundance—from the impact and value we're already delivering to the world.

Development work is grounded in organizational purpose over personal ego.

Sometimes, Executive Directors and fundraisers center themselves in donor relationships, leaning on their charisma or personal networks instead of the mission, which is a mistake.

Our job is to be stewards of the mission, the team, and the community we serve.

If a staff member leaves and a donor follows, that's a red flag. It usually means the relationship was built around an individual rather than the organization. This happens often with founders or long-time leaders experiencing "Founder's Syndrome"—the belief that everything revolves around them. Of course, over time, genuine friendships grow between staff and donors or board members. Executive and development directors should be mission-focused, with their eye on impact.

Boundaries: Show Respect for Yourself and Others

One of the most valuable lessons I've learned is that boundaries are a form of self-respect, accountability, and foster mutual understanding. Early in my career, a men's club asked me if they could deliver lox boxes (beloved packages of lox, cream cheese and bagels, also known as Jewish soul food) to a nursing home—in the middle of the night. I joked about bringing a cot. Thankfully, my boss reminded me to propose a more reasonable time. That moment taught me how easy it is to overextend—and how powerful it is to set clear expectations.

Now, I choose when to provide my services for free or when and how much to charge for services I provide. Worth isn't about title or salary—it's about owning your value.

Development can sometimes be lumped in with admin or communications. While there's overlap, each has its own distinct role. Development is strategy. Clarifying these distinctions helps everyone succeed.

Boundaries are guideposts that protect the work, preserve your energy, and keep the focus where it matters most.

Listen to Your Inner Voice:
It Knows the Way

When you're stuck, whether it's on a project or due to a technical glitch, sometimes the best move is to step away. Take a walk, do the dishes, or even sleep on it. That quiet space often unlocks the idea you need. I call this the "step-away-and-let-it-hit-you" method. It even works for finding lost things—which I know from my great knack for misplacing items.

In small nonprofit shops, we're constantly DOING, which can block creativity. But stillness (many times mistaken for procrastination) is often where ideas lives. Give yourself space to think. Intuition plays a big role too; it's the cousin of the lightning-bolt idea. As a kid walking alone, I knew when to trust my gut—and it kept me safe. When I sold shoes after college, I sensed who'd buy, even if they didn't look the part.

That same intuition guides my work today. Whether crafting fundraising strategies or creative slogans, I've learned to trust the signals I get—backed by experience and deep listening.

The final piece? Confidence. Trust your instincts, refine your ideas, and resist letting others talk you out of them. When your gut and your experience align, you're rarely wrong.

Forget Regrets or Mistakes:
Take Everything in Stride as a Learning Opportunity!

I was the child parents described as having the "just gotta" syndrome—as in, "I just gotta do this," or "I just gotta grab that" before heading off to school. I've become somewhat legendary for losing things (though I like to think of it as leaving pieces of myself in different places) and forgetting my head if it weren't attached. I recently had to buy a new paper calendar to replace the one I lost. Yes, I know—I should probably just rely on my digital calendar. My natural organizational skills are...challenged.

Growing up, I spent a lot of time searching for lost mittens and crying in the cold (Georgia cold, mind you—not Chicago cold) and being royally scolded by my parents. From these types of experiences, I've learned how to sweat the small stuff without sweating the small stuff.

That said, I'm excellent at planning events and leveraging them to advance an organization. I'm also great at meeting deadlines and working through fine details—even if some college friends remember the time I tied my hairbrush to a lamp so I could remember where it was. These days, I can plan a 500-person event without a detailed checklist, simply because I've done it so many times. Still, I'll happily create that checklist if it helps put Type A folks at ease. This kind of disheveled, creative chaos has made me highly adaptable. Nothing ever goes as planned in fundraising, and you learn to work around the unexpected. I've grown completely comfortable walking into organizational chaos and making it work as a specialty.

Once, at a dinner event, the video we had planned to show failed at the last minute. So, I invited one of the video's subjects—who, thankfully, had an acting background—to come up and speak instead. I hadn't planned for how long they'd talk, but they got the message across—just with a few more words than I'd expected.

At another dinner, there was a literal fire at the hotel, which no one attending even knew about. A bathroom ran out of toilet paper, and as the point person for the event, I found the concierge, noticed water leaking from the wall, grabbed toilet paper, handled the bathroom issue, and got back to the dinner. Just another night of putting out fires— figuratively and literally.

Then there was the time I worked as an annual giving officer for an educational institution. Our year-end mailing to Chicago alumni (most of whom lived locally) never arrived. When I called the post office, they scolded me for my ignorance in not realizing that Chicago had one of the worst mail systems in the country—when you know, you know! It felt like a massive loss at the time—potentially over $20,000 in small donations.

Luckily, the institution could absorb the hit; a smaller nonprofit might have failed as a result. I was horrified. Another time, I miscalculated the catering cost by over 100% because I underestimated how much people would drink. Had I paid a fixed amount per person instead of paying for the amount of alcohol actually consumed, I would have stayed on budget. I thought I was going to lose my job over that one. Now, I always negotiate pricing based on time or fixed cost rather than consumption.

These experiences, and many more like them, have sharpened my adaptability and my sense of humor. Any seasoned fundraiser has a catalog of war stories: donor snafus, backstage chaos, and unexpected crises. Over time, you learn to take these bumps in stride.

It's much easier to laugh when you look back. These moments have built my resilience, my instincts, and maybe even a bit of audacity. Often, the bigger risk lies in freezing up or trying to plan everything perfectly rather than just moving forward and trusting yourself to adjust.

It's Always About the Relationship

Early in my career, I realized that relationships propel philanthropy over programs and tax write-offs, even though impact is the product we are selling. Fundraising could also be a vehicle for donors to whitewash questionable business practices or build a certain kind of reputation. Many prominent families in the U.S. have used philanthropy and politics to shape the legacies and influence they seek.

At one of the first agencies I worked for in Chicago, we had a campaign where a volunteer—let's call him Frank—was incredibly helpful... some might even say pushy, depending on your perspective. He was determined to elevate the organization's campaign to the next level. If leadership had taken the time to read his paper donor file (this was back in the old-school days), they would've better understood why he was so personally invested.

I read the file—but I kept what I learned to myself. I believed in honoring the privacy of the relationship he wanted to have with the organization. That, too, is part of being a good fundraiser.

One of the first lessons in fundraising is this: it's not about the cause; it's about who's doing the asking. Frank's commitment and influence helped open doors and bring others to the table. His involvement directly contributed to the campaign's success.

Some fundraisers get swept up in the prestige, the gossip, the VIP access. They treat fundraising like a spectator sport, chasing status instead of focusing on strategic, relationship-driven work. But true fundraising is more like studying history: understanding how things connect, what people value, and what motivates them. Relationships should always be approached with care, thoughtfulness, and discretion.

And here's another truth: Gifts are often about more than pure gratitude or altruism. Some people give because they want to see their name in lights. Others want to curry favor with a business leader, impress a board, or gain entry into a social circle. Whatever the reason, if your agency benefits and the donors' motives don't compromise your mission, the "why" becomes secondary. It's still about the relationship.

If you're lucky—and diligent—you'll learn which donors want that relationship to go beyond the first gift. And if you're wise, you'll invest in that connection, because it's those lasting relationships that keep your mission alive.

Surprise Yourself with the Unexpected, Part 1

Perfection shows itself as anxiety and blocks inspiration and results.

We need to give ourselves space to make mistakes—or let the unexpected happen—and be okay with it, which is easier said than done. A young fundraiser recently asked me about perfection, and I told her: COVID cured us of that. We lost donors, yes—but we also held on to many. It reminded us of what matters: humility, humanity, and connection.

I always aim to do my best, with the goal of creating transformation and meaning over cold perfection.

The only perfect creature in my house is my cat, Finn—except when he tries to wake me at 4 a.m. for breakfast.

No dogs here, purr my special claws

Good Enough is Often Better than Perfect, Part 2

I love working with lawyers. They're often excellent perfectionists—maybe it's all that training in crafting a tight legal argument. Artists are perfectionists, too. They visualize how their work should take shape, then tweak and edit until it matches the vision in their head. Plenty of people fall into this perfectionist camp. They get stuck in their heads, waiting for things to feel just right. Perfectionism becomes a problem when it stops you from moving forward.

Like the mind-muscle connection you build at the gym, there's a mental discipline required to recognize when you're working hard out of passion versus burning energy out of anxiety. A little nervous energy is natural and constructive when you are working on something big. Anxiety can also be paralyzing and exhausting, stealing energy that should be going toward your goal.

My default approach is to act first, then think. Once I understand what's in front of me, I'm in motion. Honestly, I could stand to be more pragmatic at times—basically that is outside of my operating style. A friend imitated me channeling a little Greta Garbo energy without a care. I love this concept. (Look her up if you don't know her. She was a vibe.)

Balance is the name of the game; planning, ambition and risk-taking all need to live side-by-side. I follow my gut. And while I enjoy putting off deadlines like the next person, I like my responses to feel fresh. I think ahead, without obsession. I'm comfortable speaking extemporaneously (unless a camera is on me—then I freeze like a deer in headlights).

If you find yourself stuck in overthinking mode, take an improv class. Really. It's the best way I know to shake off that inner critic and get comfortable with the unexpected. It teaches you to say "yes" and run with it instead of getting bogged down in "no" or "maybe."

We've all got something we're working on. The key is to keep moving towards your goal one step at a time.

Finn in "Greta Garbo" mode

Saving Money vs. Spending:
Why It's Okay to Cut Flowers

I rarely spend money on flowers for events. One colleague hated that. We compromised; I bought vases and spent $50 at Mariano's. It wasn't worth it. Eventually, I swapped flowers for paper trifolds with sponsor names and org info—cheap, clear, effective.

I outsourced where I struggled, like with printing name tags. It saved time and prevented mistakes. Some hire event planners. I didn't. But I should've paid for more help. Staff hated being roped in to help with random tasks for the benefit. "Not-my-job" culture is real.

With good tools, you can run a 500-person event with a two-person team—if you plan and outsource smartly. Pay for onsite help with the paddle raises and hire a solid auctioneer.

Events are showcases. Spend where it counts. Cut where you can. That kind of judgment comes with experience—and impacts your bottom line in the best ways.

Acknowledging Others' Success Strengthens Your Own

I'm naturally competitive, so when I hear someone raised more than I did for a similar mission, I pause and remind myself to celebrate their success. I learned this from my daughter, an actor, who taught me the power of generosity when it comes to acknowledging others' wins. It makes you a better teammate and a better community member.

Fundraising is competitive because resources are scarce. However, when you begrudge others' accomplishments, it reflects more on your scarcity mindset. I've seen ideas—and even donors—lifted by organizations. To me, that kind of behavior says more about how poorly or inauthentically a cause is being run. I believe with enough strategic requests and the right messaging, I will eventually meet my goals.

There's a difference between being inspired and copying. One organization even took our tagline and made it their own—just down the street from us. I called their development director, asked how it came about, and learned a consultant handed it to them with little research. I let them know (gently) that they may have overpaid for that advice and left it at that. Just a quiet acknowledgment. Forgiven and remembered. It's all good.

Know When to Close Shop and Relax

It's about 85 degrees on a quiet summer evening in Georgia. I'm sitting in the shade at a picnic table, enjoying a snow cone. Children are playing in the dirt and mothers are chatting while keeping an eye on their little ones. After a long day of travel from Chicago, I'm finally easing into relaxation. It's the perfect way to wind down.

Throughout my career, I've helped busy lawyers carve out time for charity work. They're often overwhelmed—buried in deadlines and barely able to pause and reflect. When I overwork, I get migraines and start feeling anxious about my never-ending to-do list.

Recently, I was talking with a friend who was juggling a major job interview presentation alongside a long list of responsibilities at her current job. When she hit a wall creatively, I told her to take a walk or go work out. In other words: Stop banging your head against the wall. Give your brain a break. Often, the best ideas come when you stop trying to force them once you've started thinking about something else, like when you suddenly remember the name you were grasping for earlier.

Personally, I get some of my best ideas while washing dishes. Back when I worked at a nonprofit, I'd often credit a consultant with my ideas so that leadership would be more open to them. I knew my ideas had merit—I just also knew how to get them heard. That kind of intuitive creativity needs to be nurtured, just like physical health. Rest, movement, and mental space are essential.

Of course, relaxing in Georgia in the summer has its draw-backs—namely the bugs. Luckily, I remembered to pack bug spray and anti-itch cream.

It's Never Too Late to Step Forward

I often find myself volunteering to mentor people who are navigating career transitions. They range from recent college and law-school grads to artists, nonprofit professionals, and folks in midlife trying to reimagine their next chapter.

For those who are older, re-entering the job market can feel especially vulnerable. The process is daunting and judgmental, and can weigh heavily. Early in my career, after I'd taken a few months off to spend time with my young daughter at the time, I was questioned in a job interview about my brief pause in working. The comment struck me as unnecessary—and more telling of the interviewer than of me.

When I review someone's resume, what I look for is how they frame their story: what they've learned, built, or led. Time off is just an element of life and is a distraction from the overall assessment of qualifications.

I encourage people to treat interviews as conversations and opportunities to mutually assess fit. Now that most of my interviews are with potential clients, I see even more clearly how much chemistry and alignment matter, sometimes more than qualifications. Trusting your instincts about work culture is key. Some employers will be the wrong fit, and vice versa. That's really a form of clarity, rather than rejection.

My mentoring shifts depending on the person: For artists, I help them name and articulate their vision, so they feel more confident sharing it. For lawyers, I emphasize relationship-building—in hiring, in workplace culture, and with potential clients.

For those over 50, I offer a gentler hand. Often, they're rebuilding, and I focus on tangible, next-step strategies with encouragement to match. For fundraisers, I guide them to listen carefully to an organization's expectations. Sometimes the role amounts to the unsustainable tenet of "spinning gold from straw."

For young fundraisers and communications professionals, I push them to identify what they truly enjoy. If a development officer dislikes asking for money, or if a comms person struggles to tell a persuasive story, it may be time to change direction. In every case, the goal is the same: to affirm each person's value, elevate their confidence, and offer practical tools to help them move forward—whether they're just starting out, shifting gears, or beginning again.

Going through job searches and dealing with constant rejection is difficult enough. My role, when I can offer it, is to remind people they're more equipped than they think—and there is always time to shine.

PART II

On Founders, Organizational Struggles & Why Fundraisers Leave

The Messy Challenge of Founding a Nonprofit

Nonprofit founders are visionaries. Like artists, they begin with an idea and sculpt it into something real—not for profit, but for impact, expression, or engagement. Unlike business entrepreneurs, their return on investment is emotional, communal, or structural rather than profit.

Creating a new organization is an act of both faith and endurance. Most founders start with little more than a mission, a few supportive people, and a lot of grit. There's rarely a roadmap; it's a constant cycle of doing what's most urgent—often with too few resources or help.

Founders wear every hat. Administrative needs compete with programming, fundraising, and compliance. It's chaotic. Mistakes are common. The key is to improve as you go—learn, adjust, and maintain your legal and financial footing. The first real milestone is governance, and it's often misunderstood. I've lost count of how many times I've heard founders say they pulled bylaws off the internet and hoped for the best. Bylaws are your organization's constitution; they should reflect your specific mission, philosophy and structure. This is a place you want to avoid cutting corners by obtaining assistance from a lawyer or nonprofit advisor. Solid bylaws equip an organization to build an effective board culture and a sustainable organization for the long run.

Early boards are usually friends, colleagues, and even family. You need to be intentional from the very beginning. Skip family appointments, if you can. Find people who believe in the mission and are ready to grow with it, even if it takes you more time than you planned for.

At first, boards tend to be hands-on—stuffing envelopes and planning events. As the organization matures, the board should transform as well. Their job should shift into oversight, accountability, and support versus micromanagement.

Define roles early—founder, executive director, board member, staff, volunteer. Write job descriptions, set expectations, and create policies that evolve with your program. Everyone needs to be honest about their capacity and be open to outside help.

Donors play a critical role in early organizational life. Some are better suited than others. Donors who expect immediate polish might be a better option to tackle in the future. Be clear about what you can deliver. The right donors understand the messiness of building, while the wrong ones become unnecessary distractions.

At its best, founding an organization is a collaboration between a mission, its messenger, and a community that believes in both. You will make mistakes that facilitate your growth. Eventually, you will move beyond startup mode—likely still feeling scrappy. This is the time to invite fresh perspectives, reassess, and prepare for growth.

Founders need support: emotional, technical, and financial. And they need grace—grace to fail, to learn, and to keep going. Because great organizations are built through testing, correction, and daily acts of courage.

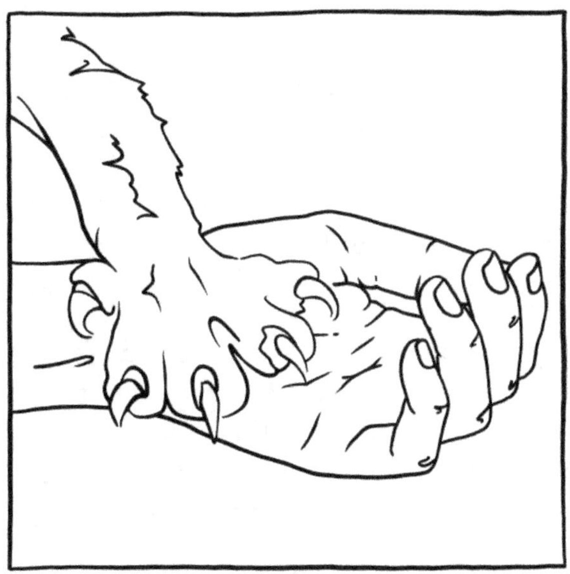

You are under a wrist

Checking the Boxes:
Why Your Paperwork Isn't Your Organizational Development Plan

I f you've got funding, a working program, and a ready team before you launch—congratulations! You're officially a unicorn.

What I see more often is this: Someone with a big heart, a good idea, and just enough knowledge to be dangerous. They find a lawyer, get three friends to join the board, download bylaws, and hit "submit." Voila—nonprofit status.

On paper? Impressive. In practice? Red flags are waving like it's a parade.

Everything looks legit. But the budget's off. One person is doing all the work. The board hasn't met in months—unless brunch counts.

Filing to become a 501(c)(3) is easy, in normal times (once that becomes the direction your research tells you to go). Building something that lasts takes real structure and patience. A nonprofit is still a business, with legal duties and financial risks.

Say you open a theater. Great. But did you think about payroll taxes? Liability insurance? That volunteer working 20 hours a week who needs to be on payroll? I've seen organizations get fined, shut down, or implode because nobody read the fine print.

And then there's fundraising. New groups often want to hire a development director with a "great Rolodex." Donors skip the stranger with a title and want to give to the person with passion, proximity, and a plan—the founder and the board.

Start small. Be clear. Build slow. Focus on one program you can do well. Find a board that shows up. Understand your finances and your capacity. "If we build it, they will come" only works if what you build doesn't leak the first time it rains.

Ask yourself:
- Do we know what we're doing—or are we just mimicking what we think nonprofits do?
- Did we do our due diligence and determine that it even makes sense to create a nonprofit?
- Can we explain what success looks like, in plain English?
- Do we have enough infrastructure to survive a minor disaster—or a major audit?

If the honest answer is "not yet," that's okay. You can go back and get it right. Think of it as your nonprofit's second draft—better ingredients, stronger bones, and fewer panic attacks.

Fundraising Starts in Your Imagination:
Slow Down for It

One of the most unexpectedly useful things I learned came from high school voice lessons. To sing well, I had to visualize the unseen muscle connections; breathing, posture, and tone all had to be balanced.

Turns out that skill—imagining what is invisible—is the key to fundraising.

Before you dive into tactics, ask: Why is this mission important? Before the programs and the budget are planned, you need a clearly defined purpose.

That "why"—your case for support—is where real fundraising begins. It takes vision, editing, and a lot of conversation. You will rework your language many, many times. This foundational step is what too many new organizations breeze over too quickly.

I've seen it over and over: An organization gets its paperwork done, builds a program, then assumes the money will follow. They call in a consultant, asking for funding plans, foundation lists, and sponsor decks.

That's when I hold up the stop sign.

Because fundraising is more than just chasing

money. It's about telling the story of why your mission matters—to you, your community, and your supporters. That conversation starts before the ask—with shared values, trust, and alignment. Think of your case for support like a strategic plan built through relationships. It's about shared purpose over internal priorities.

When your message is clear, fundraising becomes an invitation for investment versus a request for a gift. That's what builds long-term support. Success comes from starting with vision and investing in invisible steps—messaging, relationships, and honest questions. Then, you're ready to get started.

Vision First:
Light Sparks into Sustainability

> *It's a cold Sunday morning in January. I'm buried in gift tax acknowledgment letters. People believed in the mission and responded. That belief deserves a thoughtful and personalized thank you.*

I think about what it takes to start something meaningful. Especially now, with burnout and political chaos in the air. It takes courage—the kind artists, activists, and founders summon daily. What I hear about from them most often is fear: fear of doing it wrong, fear of being seen too soon—or not at all—and fear of success.

Mindset matters. Vision means seeing what has yet to exist. That's hard to explain when you're building the plane as you fly—or when your idea is still more feeling than structure.

The answer: **Begin anyway**.

Many founders light the match just to see what happens. Sometimes it catches—and they're suddenly leading a real program. But the program needs infrastructure to continue or the flame will burn out.

Too often, founders are left alone. And without support, one of two things happens:
1. They doubt themselves and stop asking for help, or
2. the organization becomes about them, and collapses when they leave.

Both are avoidable, with honesty, planning, and a shift from founder-centered to mission-centered thinking.

Just like my voice lessons where I had to imagine the muscle connection, I encourage founders to visualize the emotional core of their mission.

Why are we doing this? Who is it for? Why does it matter now?

That leads to understanding that brings about connection.

The real work begins before the ask. Develop a message that people want to join in on as investors, rather than just as donors. When fundraising is built on relationships and purpose, it becomes transformational rather than transactional. People end up giving time, ideas, and skills—in addition to dollars.

Build the Organization to Outlive You

When founders stay in survival mode, the mission stays tethered to them. That's risky. You need to build something that can grow beyond you.

That means:

- Custom bylaws that reflect your mission
- A strategic board—beyond friends and family
- Clear roles and expectations
- Succession planning from day one
- Asking for help when needed

You'll miss things. The best leaders learn and adapt. Hold onto your original vision—and let it grow. The real sign of impact?

When your idea thrives without you in every room. Before you chase the money or polish the org chart, sit with your "why." Imagine what's possible. Build from that. Invite people in. Take the risk.

Board Relations &
Organizational Survival:
Be Ready to Crack Some Eggs

I magine a board that says it has no responsibility for finances or governance. Unheard of, if an organization is to survive.

In one case, a board president fired the board—by mail. Legal? No. But it got their attention. They called a meeting and voted him out. He didn't regret it. "At least they did something."

Boards often go quiet when stakes are high. The problems cannot fix themselves. A board has legal and financial duties. And silence is deadly.

Board service is another job. If you care enough to lend your name, lend your backbone, too. Sometimes, to make changes on your board, you've got to crack a few eggs. Bring the frying pan and some seasoning.

Why Development Leaders Often Leave

I shared comical event mishaps earlier (*See Part I: Forget Regrets and Mistakes—and Take Everything in Stride as a Learning Opportunity!*) But what about behind the scenes? The internal strife I've seen leaves little to laugh about. Fundraisers carry the weight quietly—fixing broken systems and smiling through dysfunction. We stay hopeful, hanging on for the next retreat or reset.

We believe in the mission. That's why we keep going.

Until we don't.

This quiet endurance can become enabling. And when we finally leave, we most often do it gracefully—with a "thank you for the opportunity." I've made a career fixing broken parts of nonprofits—structural and interpersonal. And I've learned that sometimes, the wisest move is to walk away.

Leaving the industry helped me see my real strength: helping people in tough transitions. I bring calm to chaos and transparency to confusion. Change takes time. Fundraisers see the cracks before others do. If you've outgrown your organization's vision, it might be time to change ships—or roles. That kind of change creates growth for you and for the mission.

PART III

Dealing with Society's Distrust of Nonprofit Idealism

The Tragedy of Cancel Culture and Its Impact on Fundraising

undraisers are salespeople with a mission. We work with all kinds of people who invest in our causes. We don't have to agree with their politics; we just need to find shared values that reflect the missions we serve.

A friend of mine was blackmailed by a donor simply for listing their pronouns. It wasn't political, but the donor made it so. During the pandemic, I hosted an event that required proof of a negative COVID test. Some guests refused. It was disturbing. Nonprofit leaders now face strident, demoralizing, and sometimes absurd confrontations. The work has always required resilience. Today's climate adds an extra burden.

While many of us have learned how to deflect conflict, the erosion of trust in public institutions—education, medicine, religion, the post office—makes our jobs more complex and difficult. Nonprofit institutions that are far from perfect are meant to serve the greatest good instead of meeting the impossible standards set by the loudest critics.

It's getting harder to gain new donors. That makes our donor relationships even more precious. As fundraisers, we have the responsibility—and opportunity—to build bridges across deep divides.

We're heading into a storm of division and distrust. Staying in public service—especially in nonprofits—is now an act of quiet activism. I hope the next generation still chooses this work, despite the growing challenges. Service remains a powerful form of hopeful resistance.

The meeting can start now

Defining Activism Through a Nonprofit Corporate Structure

I recently met with a startup nonprofit whose executive committee existed only on paper. There's a movement to reject traditional nonprofit structures in favor of community power. While compelling in theory, I struggle with it in practice. Someone still must be responsible for the overall policymaking and operations of the organization—or more basically, keeping the lights on.

I often challenge authority and think outside the box. However, I also champion the idea that you need structure to provide something to measure your progress toward reaching goals. Engagement can still be innovative within an organizational structure.

As a quiet activist and strategist—often the front-line diplomat—I'm always seeking new approaches. I found Restorative Justice Circles as spaces for listening. You bring your experience and make space for others to bring theirs. (I'm referring to circles used for community-building, rather than conflict resolution.)

What if we applied that model more broadly? Imagine debates built on listening instead of winning, where we ask people why they believe what they do. We might find unexpected common ground—and perhaps a path forward.

I think of a story I read recently, about conservative mothers in Tennessee grieving children lost to a school shooting who felt ignored by their state legislature. Regardless of politics, how do you not empathize with grieving parents fighting for community safety? Why are lawmakers dismissing them—not just as constituents, but as women and mothers?

When we reward the loudest over those who quietly seek understanding, we all lose.

When Kids Lead Change, What Other Burdens Do We Add?

I n college sociology, I learned that it was youth who made school desegregation possible. But did they have the emotional support they needed in the process? I think of the Black children of the 1950s and '60s who faced harassment just for integrating schools. Was the pride of progress and strength faced in adversity enough to help them carry the burden of pain they endured?

I've been reflecting on my childhood—and the quiet burdens of being a kid shaped by adult convictions. Dad used to say, "I can write a letter and make it better." We learned early: complain, and you might end up in a protest.

In the mid-'70s in public school, we had school prayer each morning. My father, in classic form, wrote a letter citing the separation of church and state. So, as a first- or second-grader, I sat in the hallway during prayer. Teachers asked what I did wrong. I had to explain every day. I wasn't for or against it; I was a rule-follower. It just didn't seem fair to be singled out.

Then, there was the time a girl named Candle broke my glasses in the first grade. The teacher sent a note home accusing me of letting her wear them. My parents were ignorant of my ability to read at this point. I read the note, panicked, and tossed it into a creek. I wasn't accepting a spanking for something I didn't do, especially not over those ugly glasses. (My eyeglasses style improved when I started working at 16 years old and bought my own.)

In high school, I made it to the next level in a debate contest, but I was bumped from the team for a politician's son. It was sexist and infuriating, so I quit. Dad made me write a memo to the school board, and the coach was removed as a result. I hated the confrontation and I didn't want to fight this battle in this way.

Once, a Shoney's restaurant blocked the sidewalk during renovations, so Dad had to cross the street. He wrote to corporate headquarters stating that his life was being "endangered." They sent two meal vouchers to appease him. My brother and I used them gladly.

Now, in my 50s, I choose my battles carefully. I prefer working behind the scenes—not always as the front-facing fighter my hippie father was. Still, I call things as I see them. I'm patient—until I'm not.

Simplicity is Centered in the Face of Adversity

In a world that feels like it's unraveling—communities, institutions, families—it's easy to lose sight of what matters. When things feel overwhelming, I return to simplicity. I focus on beauty, meaning, and grace.

Give freely. Help without expectation. Stay grounded.

In my neighborhood, kids still play outside. I recently cleaned up my daughter's old wagon and gifted it to my young neighbors. Watching them play brought me quiet joy.

Just recently, a three-year-old neighbor asked their mom to share some birthday cake with me. They ran out, jumping with excitement as I accepted. Their mom said it was entirely their idea. I told the older kids I'd gladly ruin my dinner for birthday cake. I was touched.

Today, I drove over an hour to volunteer at a community garden in Englewood, a neighborhood on the south side of Chicago. A North Carolina farmer now teaches neighbors how to grow food. I worked alongside strangers, who quickly became something more, all of us connected by purpose.

Sometimes, all I offer is a nod or smile. But even that brings peace.

When the world feels heavy, I ground myself: tending my garden, watching for hummingbirds, walking, calling a friend. These are small acts of faith. They help me move forward with purpose. That, to me, is the best use of my time and energy. A better tomorrow begins with kindness today.

Fight for What you Know is Right. When You Give Up Hope, You Lose.

No matter your politics, the rise of autocracy in America is alarming. There's a collective unease—driven by economic anxiety, rising homelessness, global instability, and a culture of cancellation from all sides.

When someone tells me they feel hopeless, I suggest something simple and positive. Start small. I grew up in the South, where you hold doors open for people. In Chicago, it surprises some. Occasionally, someone refuses to accept my offer of an open door, but most smile and say thank you. I greet people on the street—in that habitual small-town way; Chicago is just a bigger version of one. My family wishes I were a bit more reserved, but it's hard to change someone who is hard-wired to feel they are rarely surrounded by strangers. These interactions also sharpen my intuition—I know when something feels off.

Connecting with people always matters. I show up for others. I meet them for coffee. I help with résumés. It reminds me of our shared humanity, especially when the world feels cold and sometimes dangerous.

Start with one person. Make a difference. Support organizations that help build community. When you fight, you win.

PART IV

My Path to Becoming a Confident Leader, an Example

What Have I Learned About Community Engagement?

Community engagement is more than just reflecting demographics or offering services you think are helpful. It's active listening—an ongoing dialogue that invites real give-and-take. And it's easy to get it wrong. The key is listening deeply and responding—thoughtfully rather than reactively—to what people believe is appropriate or needed. "Community" can mean many things to many people.

Each time I visit my hometown, I stop by a favorite Thai restaurant, and I nearly always run into someone who knew my family. The town has grown a lot in the 30+ years since I left, but that kind of long memory reminds me how deep-rooted real engagement is.

When I walk through any Chicago neighborhood, I think about the families who live there—the schools, churches, and gathering places that hold it together. Real engagement, especially in professional settings, means honoring the long-standing relationships and investments people have made in their communities. These bonds form over decades. That's a lesson I carry into my volunteer work and political life in Chicago.

In my current neighborhood, I stay politically active. Most of us want the same basic things: for our children to be safe—for them to play outside and sit on the front steps without fear.

It breaks my heart when kids can't play outside safely. Undoing generations of disinvestment and systemic barriers means seeing every neighborhood as part of our shared community, without artificial boundaries or judgment.

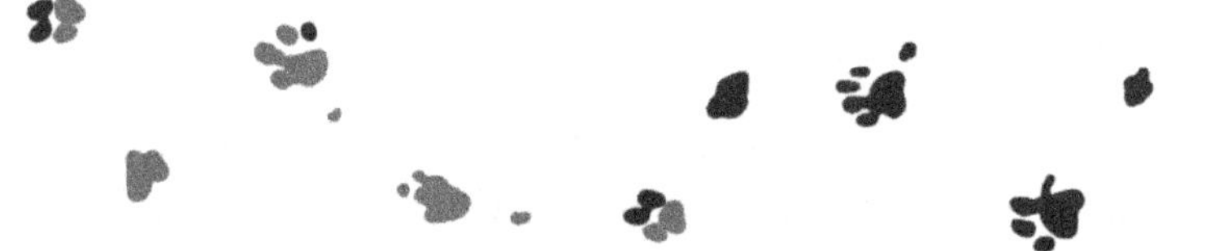

I'm Grateful for Social Justice Advocacy

For the past three years, I've served as a delegate to a national convention for a human rights organization, representing my hometown. By now, I am a familiar presence to those with a sharp visual memory. Each year, I feel more at home; I'm deeply moved by the speeches, the elders, the youth, and the relentless volunteers who keep this movement alive.

One thing I've noticed: We're good at waiting. Whether it's for a plenary session, a speaker, or a luncheon, there's a gracious patience that connects us. When President Biden came to speak, we waited over three hours and no one complained. People laughed, talked, danced in the aisles. It was beautiful.

One morning as we waited for a session to begin, a man with a thick East Coast accent pulled out a clarinet. He'd taught himself to play after retiring and now brought it everywhere. He played gentle folk tunes by artists such as Simon & Garfunkel or Peter, Paul & Mary. A fellow retiree and former musician offered tips. Then, the clarinetist broke into a loud singing rendition of "House of the Rising Sun," with full commitment. His audience thinned quickly.

I leaned over and asked, "So... does your wife like your practicing?" Without missing a beat, he replied, "She hates it. That's why I play anywhere else I can."

That exchange summed up the convention's spirit: casual, generous, and welcoming. I had dozens of these small, lovely conversations there. My lack of shyness is often met with warmth.

I'm proud to be part of something historic, vital, and alive. This is where I feel most grounded in the work of building the world I want to see. I've learned more through my advocacy work than I ever did as a history major at Northwestern University or growing up in Georgia. It's grounded me. We all need to step back, listen, and learn. And when the moment calls for it, we need to stand up.

Political Participation:
Nostalgia from the 1992 NYC DNC Convention

Now seems like the perfect time to share my 1992 DNC adventure in New York City. I was 21, hoping to catch up with a friend who had officially volunteered for the convention and aimed to obtain a job in D.C. I flew to NYC with just a backpack, a dream, and a place with my grandfather to crash. Somehow, I caught up with my friend and snuck into speeches, parties, and events. At one point, I saw two older women on the street; one wore a sunhat flopping every which way. I thought, "Southerners!" and asked to tag along. It turned out they too were crashing the convention. We ended up walking in a parade and spotted NYC Mayor David Dinkins getting into a limo. Naturally, we followed.

We passed bleachers full of cheering young people. The women I was crashing with wanted to sit, but police told us the seats were reserved for people with AIDS. That was my first real exposure to the HIV/AIDS advocacy movement.

We kept walking. Soon, we saw Mayor Dinkins get out of the limo and head into a building. We entered the building and tried to follow him through the same door—until someone informed us it was the men's bathroom. We let him have his privacy.

Eventually, we snuck into the Minority Mayors Caucus. I saw Rosa Parks with her niece. Spike Lee was there, too. My favorite moment? Spotting a woman I'd shared a cab with earlier; she worked for Clinton's Arkansas team and had been a bit arrogant. Waving at her with a giant grin was especially satisfying.

Even my Republican grandfather in Chicago later claimed he spotted me on TV watching Governor Mario Cuomo deliver a masterful speech. The whole experience was electric.

PART V

Tanya, the Vanity Reel Journal *(Write your own, too. Positive introspection is a gift that fuels your work.)*

Creatively Approaching Life

Quoting the immortal Little Richard: "I'm not conceited, I'm convinced." Or in modern terms: I feel sorry for anyone who tries to train me.

It's no accident that I hate sitting in one place and being lectured or told what to do. Reading instructions? Pass. Show me a picture and I'll improvise. I'll imagine the logic I need to get through a database—sometimes crashing it more than once, as a result—but I'll figure out the answers on my own terms. And if you're in my way? You might want to move.

Take the poor volunteer who co-led a Restorative Justice Circle with me. About 30 seconds in, she realized I didn't need a co-lead. I nodded graciously and told her: "I know. But I'm glad you figured it out."

The circle mirrored all the best parts of fundraising: When you give, you receive.

You can offer me pointers without interfering with my finesse. I'll do it my own messy way—and that's the fun of it.

Creatives have their own rhythm. We color outside the lines because we see patterns others might miss. I've learned to be more patient with those who need structure—and more suspicious of those trying to impose it on me. Grace of space? That's the real gift.

Finn's glamour shot!

"The Legend"
I'll Wear the T-Shirt

Once, I stepped in as interim development director of a charity while the Executive Director recovered from an illness. I rebuilt staff, supported the board, and planned their first post-pandemic in-person benefit. We raised a significant amount of money; the executive director came back strong, and staff were promoted from within. A total win from my perspective.

Fast forward two years later. My daughter meets the organization's celebrity benefactor and says, "You must know my mother, Tanya." The benefactor replies, "You mean the legend?"

Naturally, my daughter realized I'd never let her live that down. She was right. For Mother's Day, she gifted me a purple t-shirt that says "The Legend." It's now a favorite, along with my "Women Belong in Charge" tee. My husband just shakes his head and says, "Raygun (an Iowa-derived T-shirt slogan company) really knows their customer."

He's not wrong. I LOVE being a Legend.

Aiming with Confidence

This quote headlined my 8th-grade Optimist Oratorical contest speech. My classmates could recite it with me by heart from all my practice. Shout-out to my endlessly patient language arts teacher, Mrs. Manring. Sorry to my eighth-grade class who had to put up with the constant practice. I ended up losing the contest to a cute girl with braids and crutches who won the sympathy vote. My delivery and speech were sharper. First lesson: People vote with their hearts over their minds. As a fundraiser, that lesson has paid off in dividends.

Years later, I took the Myers-Briggs and found my leadership style is eerily close to Napoleon's (strategic genius side rather than the tyrannical side). I just know who I am. When you move forward with self-confidence, you move differently than when you question your instincts.

I'm direct, open, and deeply invested in helping others succeed. Mentorship is impact multiplied. I thrive in boundaryless environments over rigid hierarchies built to maintain control. While I have patience with people who need to learn, I move around people who put up artificial barriers that get in my way. Why am I going on about myself? Because if you want to overcome real obstacles—internal or external—you need to know who you are. I chase outcomes, not approval. And it works.

My Choice of Flea Bag Motels:
A Character Study

I recently stayed at the Ritz-Carlton in Naples, Florida. It was lovely—gracious staff, perfect espresso—and I delightedly shared war stories with others about the worst hotels I had experienced. Case in point: a Pennsylvania motel near a truck stop, with sex trafficking busts nearby. My daughter begged me never to return. I did. Alone. The door didn't lock and I got a new room. The next room had two sketchy entrances. I was tired, but it was paid for—so I stayed!

Or the Boston room with a shared bathroom—$100 a night. A coughing, naked woman in a towel greeted me at check-in. It was still peak COVID. She didn't respond well when I introduced myself. There was the $70 room in my hometown—mid-renovation, dumpsters outside, a hot tub in the center of the room (no thanks). And my masterpiece: a $100 D.C. room so sketchy that even I said "nope." I fled and paid $230 elsewhere—a new price threshold for hotels I look for on the East Coast.

Public transit? Love it. Walking? Prefer it. Once I stayed on a NYC train where a man kept lighting his thumb like a candle to lull himself to sleep. He wasn't hurting anyone—until someone yelled at him. I was more upset with the yeller. I stayed because I had already paid for the fare.

I probably inherited all this from my bohemian, artistic, and broke '70s parents. I know I should evolve. I also have expensive taste in a favorite Chicago designer. We all have our priorities.

Addendum: I have limits. Roach choruses must stay outside.

Died & Gone to Heaven Chicken

My favorite recipe, created by me. (If you're not including a personal recipe in your memoir, what are you even doing?)

Ingredients:
2 small chickens (3–4 lbs. each)
1 lemon, halved
1 onion, halved
Fresh chopped garlic & ginger
Olive oil
Balsamic vinegar or white wine
Favorite spice blend (New Orleans-style is mine)

Directions:
Wash and prep the chickens. Skin stays on.
Preheat oven to 450°F.
Stuff with lemon and onion.
Tuck ginger and garlic under the skin.
Rub with oil, drizzle balsamic or white wine, season well (Cajun spices are one of my favorites.)
Roast for 1 hour. At 30 mins, toss in veggies.

While it cooks, prep a fresh salad and feel fancy.
Leftovers? Incredible in a salad the next day.
Improvised meals are how I roll. This will help me remember one of my favorites that I love to share.

Conclusion:
It's Serious, After All

I started this book as a checklist, with humor as my lens. Humor softens hard truths. As I wrote, I kept returning to deeper threads: dissonance, power, systems, and how good intentions get derailed by old norms.

A central lesson: Support and empowerment are different. In nonprofit and philanthropic spaces, we must question systems that reward polish over purpose, scale over substance, and familiarity over impact.

We need to lead with direction over fear. Philanthropy sets societal priorities, influences what is funded, and improves lives where it can.

Let's always question what we define as leadership and value. Center trust where impact already exists rather than what is most comfortable.

Humor got me started. Reflection carried me through.

Reflection, at its best, leads to reimagining and reinvigoration.

The End.

ABOUT THE AUTHOR

Tanya Pietrkowski is a Chicago-based fundraising strategist who helps small and mid-size nonprofits grow with purpose and strength. Founder of **TP Strategies, LLC,** she brings humor, candor, and decades of experience to her work. The UNSEEN Fundraiser is her first book—an essay collection celebrating the art, grit, and grace of small-shop fundraising.

MANIFESTAR CON CONCIENCIA

21 DIAS PARA CREAR DESDE LA INTENCIÒN Y LA PRESENCIA

Elvira Sombra

www.ingramcontent.com/pod-product-compliance
Lightning Source LLC
Chambersburg PA
CBHW071458130726
47997CB00006B/2394